An Erasmus Year Abr

Matthew Hep

ISBN 978 1 326 91489 9

Published by Lulu

ABOUT THE AUTHOR

Matthew is a student of French and European Studies at Nottingham Trent University. He started his year abroad blog *yearinfranceblog.wordpress.com* in October 2015 as he prepared to go on his year abroad in August 2016. This book contains the majority of the posts he wrote from the beginning in 2015 to the end of his year abroad in 2017.

For Matthew's year abroad, he studied as an Erasmus student at the Université de Franche-Comté in Besançon, France.

ACKNOWLEDGEMENTS

My year abroad and my academic studies would not have been possible without the support and love from my parents. To my girlfriend, who I can't thank enough – you have helped me every step of the way. To my year abroad coordinator in Besançon who was on hand to solve everything from a timetable clash to missing an exam.

All I can say is, thank you for being there. I am blessed to have such wonderful people in my life. I dedicate this book to you; those who got me through it.

BEFORE FRANCE

Décisions, décisions et bien, beaucoup de décisions
OCTOBER 28, 2015

My first year abroad meeting…

So, it's nearly the end of October 2015 and I'm already getting ready for the 'pièce de résistance' of my degree: my year abroad. I've just come out of a two hour lecture about it and to put it simply, I'm drained. I've taken in so much information and yet, I feel no closer to making a decision on a) where I want to go in France b) what I want to do. But, surely that's all the fun of it? Despite feeling slightly overwhelmed by the prospects and anxious for what could happen whilst I'm in France, I'm generally excited because I know I'll develop as a person despite making mistakes along the way. My French should get better (fingers crossed) and yes, simple things such as finding transport, buying food and just learning to live is going to be a bit of a challenge but you know what, I'm not going to let that scare me too much. I can only gain from this experience. I mean, I say all this in a somewhat privileged position (I have my usual cosy spot in the uni library and France seems far less intimidating to me at the moment but I'm not sure how I will feel this time next year…)

Maybe I should speak more about this meeting I've just had. It was interesting for quite a few reasons. Before going in, I thought, I know what I want to do. I want to be a Language Assistant in a French school teaching English. Simple. But now, I am well, a little unsure of what I want to do. I listened to a student who has just come back from spending a year in a German school and he didn't sound too positive about his experience to be honest. His location was too rural, he lived too far from his friends and he said, his German didn't improve as much as he had hoped compared to people who went to a German university. Therefore, now I am unsure of what I want to. Do I really want to stand in front of class of French kids and teach English? Can I even be a good teacher? And, then there is the question on finding my own accommodation which does sound daunting….How ever will I understand all those French rental ads? I think it's clear to say, I am confused and I have lots of questions at this early stage but like I said, I am bound to have and the process will be 'as clear as mud' until I get more information and I doubt that anything is going to make sense now.

Having said all that, it was a really useful meeting and even if it does make things harder. I would rather have these dilemmas now rather than when I'm in France. We were told that there are lots of forms to be filled in and the deadlines so, that's something that I have now got to concentrate on in order to make my life and my stress levels for that matter a little better.

Résumé en français:

Aujourd'hui j'ai eu ma première réunion à ce qui concerne mon année en France. Si je suis honnête, je suis un peu fatigué parce que j'ai appris beaucoup de choses sur mon temps en France l'année prochaine.

Je sais que je dois faire des décisions importantes dès maintenant. J'ai besoin de choisir ce que je voudrais faire; soit je devrais travailler ou étudier et également la région de la France que j'aimerais habiter. Sans aucun doute, ces décisions sont pénibles mais bien sûr, c'est attendu!

Après avoir passé son année en Allemagne, un étudiant a parlé à nous sur son expérience. Il était un assistant de langue à une école allemande. C'était le travail que je voulais faire cependant, malheureusement après avoir écouté à son épreuve, j'ai été convaincu que peut-être, je n'aimerais pas travailler à une école française. Aussi, il a dit qu'il ne pouvait pas choisir sa région parce que The British Council vous met dans une institution qui a besoin de vous. Il a expliqué que sa ville était trop petite et donc, il n'y avait pas d'activités à faire.

First stage: It's all in the prep
OCTOBER 29, 2015

It's the morning after my first year abroad meeting and, I suppose now is a great opportunity to start thinking about what I want to do in France. Even though, I still need to make vital decisions on what I actually want to do etc., I think a good place to begin is reading what past students have done.

My university has put together a map of Europe and has pinpointed where former students have been and what they did whilst they were there. What's more, students have written a page full of useful information such as accommodation, modules to do (if I plan to go to uni in France), the local area, what to do and not do, transport, how to get there and other handy tips. Using this map will definitely play some part in helping me to consider exactly what I want to do and where I want to go. So, that's my next stage; I should have a look at the map and get an insight into what others have to say and then, maybe I'll have a better idea and understanding of how I want my year abroad to go – it's all in the prep!

Résumé en français:

C'est le lendemain après la réunion et je suppose que c'est maintenant l'occasion pour penser à ce que je veux faire en France. Bien que, j'aie besoin de considérer beaucoup de choses importantes. Je crois que un bon début serait lire ce que les anciens étudiants ont fait.

Mon université a produit une carte d'Europe et elle indique où les étudiants ont habité et leur rôle (étudiant, assistant ou emploi). En outre, les étudiants ont écrit une page sur l'hébergement, les cours, la région/la ville, les choses à faire et pas à faire, le transport et le voyage – c'est très utile!

Donc, personnellement, Il faut que je lise ce que les autres disent et puis, peut-être j'aurai une meilleure idée. La préparation est essentielle!

Weighing it up
OCTOBER 30, 2015

Deciding on what to do on your year abroad is a real challenge so, I thought that it would be a good idea to weigh up all my options and give a personal opinion on them. Not only to help me decide but also, to potentially help you as well.

Options available to me:

1. Go to a French university

2. Be a Language Assistant in a French school

3. Work Placement

As you can see, I have three options to choose from. What will it be? Well, hopefully, this post will evaluate each based on my opinion.

1. Go to a French university:

Pros:

- Your university will have partner universities in France – you don't need to find a university, you can pick from a list of universities that your university has links with.

- Accommodation can be found through the university – halls of residence on campus or accommodation around the area. The university might even send you relevant information about where to find accommodation (one less thing to worry about!)

- Living in halls of residence means you are likely to live with other French or international students – this will be a great opportunity to immerse yourself in the language and improve your French.

- Being on campus in France also enables you to be fully immersed in the language – lectures will be taught in French.

- Social events – if you go to a French university, it could be easier to find out what social events are happening. Also, it could be a great opportunity to meet people and network – go to parties, societies etc.

- Many campuses are located in cities so, you will be surrounded by amenities, transport and things to do etc. You are less likely to get bored.

- Erasmus grant

- You can go home during holidays.

Cons:

- Cost of living – going to university will be expensive. The area you go to can determine the cost. Nice for example is an expensive city.

- Lots of work – you will be required to attend lectures and complete work. Will there be time to socialise? Maybe not.

- The lectures will be taught in French – this is an obvious point and yes, it is a really good thing but you will have to be prepared that it will be difficult. Will you understand enough?

- Your only money is from the Erasmus grant and money from Student Finance England.

- Will it add to your CV?

Language Assistant:

Pros:

- Salary – this is a clear advantage and benefit that being a Language Assistant brings. Being paid and the fact that you are paid relatively well, means that you will have money to do more leisure activities – socialise, travel etc. Life will be a bit easier.

- A chance to gain a unique opportunity

- A great thing to add to your CV – you can tell people that you have taught in a school yet alone, a foreign one is likely to impress not only people you meet but future employers as well.

- You can pick a preference of the age of the pupils you will teach

- Chance to see how a French school operates

- Improve your French by being surrounded by it – talk to other colleagues in French. If you go to a French upper school, you may be able to experience and learn how French is spoken by younger people – improves your vocabulary, expands your linguistic register.

- Have freedom to teach English to non-native speakers.

- School holidays

Cons:
- You will have to find your own accommodation

- The Language Assistant job is organised through the British Council. Consequently, you can only choose a region to work in rather than a specific town or city. You could be placed in a small town or you could have to commute. You just don't know where you will be working. You may end up living in a remote place.

- Some schools may want you to teach a specific topic in English which means you would have to be prepared to teach anything.

- You could be teaching in front of 30 children on your own.
Teaching English all day may mean that you don't get to practise as much French as you would like. Especially, if you teach upper school students.

- Teaching smaller children English will require you to speak more French – which is a plus as long as you can explain English grammar, English words in French to smaller children for them to understand.

Work Placement:

This option is something I have far less knowledge about because it is something I'm not too keen on doing. The reason for that is because it is much harder to do because you are required to find the work placement yourself. Speaking personally, my university doesn't help students find work placements, it is entirely up to the student and they are responsible.

The work placement is ideal for anyone who has connections in France or if they know people who work in France or run their own business in France. This makes the process much simpler.

Also, the university will have to approve the work place you are going to do and, again, speaking on behalf of my uni, they are less likely to approve jobs that may not enable you to speak enough French. Also, they won't approve jobs such as babysitting and being a waiter/waitress for the year. After my meeting this week (28th October 2015), we were told that the Erasmus grant is very tight and they won't hand out money to people who may not be doing a job that allows them to practise their French or will benefit them in some way.

There are many advantages to the work placement such as being paid, add to your CV, flexibility, and go where you want in France etc. However, at the same time, it is not an easy option and requires you to do a lot of things before hand such as finding the work, getting a contract, getting accommodation etc.

A change of heart – changer d'avis!
NOVEMBER 6, 2015

It's been just over a week since I had the first meeting on the year abroad. If you have read my last post Weighing it up, you would have seen that I listed the pros and cons of going to university, being a Language Assistant or doing a work placement.

Since writing Weighing it up, I have done a lot of thinking of what route I would like to take. And, I believe writing the post and talking to friends and family, has helped me to make a decision.

So, I have decided that going to a French university would be best and ideal for me. There are many reasons for this. Simply, I think that I will make a great deal of progress in French because I will be around the language all the time. Also, I think going somewhere where there are other young people will be a good way of networking.

I have a list of universities and at some point this week, I will look at them to see if one picks my fancy. It might be helpful to get in contact with my lecturers or other students to hear their thoughts. I know that some of my lecturers are from the cities that my university has links with so, it would be great to know a local person's perspective on the area.

I'll keep you informed on what university I eventually pick…

Résumé en français:

Il y a une semaine je suis allé à la réunion sur mon année en France. Si vous-avez lu mon post Weighing it up, vous-auriez vu que j'ai fait la liste des avantages et désavantages de l'université, l'assistante de langue et l'emploi.

Après avoir écrit le post, j'ai considéré beaucoup de choses; soit l'université est un bon choix soit l'assistante de langue. En fait, sans aucun doute, le post m'a aidé avec ma décision et aussi j'ai parlé à mes parents et mes amis.

Donc, je voudrais aller à l'université française parce que je trouve que ce sera idéal pour moi. Cet endroit améliorer mon français et je peux socialiser avec les jeunes.

J'ai une liste d'universités que je peux choisir. Je devrais contacter mes profs ou les étudiants parce que puis, je peux écouter à leur avis sur une ville où l'université a l'associée.

Pondering over the Provence
NOVEMBER 11, 2015

Today, I feel I've made some progress in deciding what university I want to go to in France. I'm not 100% sure yet, but I've definitely found a potential university I would like to study in.

I spoke to one of my lecturers this afternoon and she gave me some good information about each of our partner universities in France. I was really pleased when I found out that we had a partner university with Aix-Marseille Université. I have been to Aix-en-Provence twice for a holiday and it's an incredible place. It's a city in the South of France, in the Provence region. From what I experienced, it's was a modern, cosmopolitan city yet, it was old and traditional at the same time. It's a city which has retained the French feel you see on television. When I was there, there was a food market on the square in the mornings and, it was just so quintessentially French. I loved staying there. What's more, you are not far from the stunning Provence countryside: the acres of grapevines, the mountains, and the lavender fields and of course, the blue skies and sun.

So, when my lecturer began telling me about this university, I was actually quite excited. I would love to study in this city because I've been here and I have some idea of what it might be like. Although, I'm totally aware that studying and living here will be very different to when I was there on holiday. But, nonetheless, I know that it is a really nice place to go and it has good transport links. When I went, I flew to the airport in Marseille and then it was only 20-30 minutes by car to where we were staying which was just outside the city-centre of Aix-en-Provence. This is a real advantage for me because it means it makes travelling home (back to the UK) easier. In addition, I know of two train stations in Aix, one serving Aix with the TGV which is really handy because I could travel to other parts of France including Paris.

Since I don't know exactly where the university is in Aix-en-Provence, I did Google map the area and the university does look very nice. It looked modern and it was located in what seemed to be a quiet, residential area of the city.

From this post, it probably seems as if I have made up my mind but, I still need to do some reading up on it. I also feel I should speak to my language assistant who comes from a university in Besançon. I would like to know more about that university as well before I make any decisions. Though, from what my lecturer said today, Aix-Marseille Université seems to be ticking the boxes in terms of the location and what I can do there. Furthermore, when I visited Aix, it always seemed an incredibly safe city which is reassuring for a student.

So, unfortunately the time is not yet for me to announce where I am going....still need to ponder over it.

Bound for Besançon
NOVEMBER 16, 2015

An awful lot has changed (again) since my last post Pondering over the Provence. I thought the university in Aix-en-Provence would be the one I was going to go to. However, as I mentioned in Pondering over the Provence, I thought it would be a good idea to speak with my language assistant who studies at a university in Besançon. I didn't want to decide on Aix without considering all my options just in case I missed a really good opportunity. And, I'm so pleased I went to speak to my language assistant because my mind has well and truly changed.

After writing my last post about Aix, I emailed my language assistant to organise a meeting about Besançon because I wanted to find out her personal point of view of the university and the place in general. The meeting went really well. It lasted around an hour and a half and we spoke about a lot. I asked important questions on areas I was concerned about such as how I could get there etc.

After the hour or so, I was convinced and I still am that this is the university I want to go to. We looked on Google Maps and she showed me the area. She told me it was a lovely place and it is not too big or too small, it has loads of amenities and things to do. I feel that because the city centre is not too big, I will be able to find my way around without getting lost etc. As well, I can be close to everything I need. From what she told me and from what I saw, it looked a beautiful place. The university looked really good as well. It is right in the heart of the city centre of Besançon; in fact it reminded me a little bit of the school in the film Les Choristes!

So, I'll tell you some of the topics we spoke about.

To get there: The easiest way for me would be to fly to either Strasbourg or Basel (which is in Switzerland). And, the good thing is, I can fly from Luton which is an airport not far from where I live back home. Also, Stansted is an option. There are two train stations so, travelling on the TGV from Paris is also an option. Visiting other places in France is just as simple too.

The city: The language assistant explained to me everything that the city has to offer. It sounds a great place to live. It has lovely parks and rivers and it is a very green city. There are cinemas, supermarkets, and a weekly food market. As well, she told me that the city is renowned for its cultural heritage and owing to the university, there is a mix of nationalities, making it a diverse place to study. There is a big student community.

Accommodation: My language assistant showed me several useful websites to help me find accommodation in Besançon. She said that the city centre is the best place to live because it is where everything happens and so, I wouldn't have to pay to use public transport to find things to do. She told me to look on www.leboncoin.fr (this website can also be found under the Useful Websites tap on the homepage) to find somewhere to live. I can live by myself or do a 'colocation' which is when you share with other people. She said it would be really good to do this and live with other Erasmus students/international students or French students. I think this will be a good idea as well because a) it means I won't get lonely and b) I can speak French.

My language assistant explained to me about Facebook groups and websites to help me meet people and/or find accommodation. Speaking to her was really beneficial because she has lived there for around four years so, she knows the area very well. She said she can help me in my enquiries and also, ways to meet new people. Moreover, she told me tips and information that I think only a person who has lived there would know such as the fact that the university has restaurants in different parts of the city so you can buy your meals for something like 3.00€. We spoke briefly about banks because I wanted to know what I would have to do to set up a French bank account and what bank to go with.

I think as the months go on, I'll found out more and more. But, I'm really pleased I had the meeting with her because she answered everything I wanted to know in order to make the right decision. It is always handy when you have a native to talk to. I feel much more confident now and I am looking forward to it. I think that it will be a great place to go to. My language assistant has settled my nerves because it doesn't look so daunting now. And, even better, she has helped me to decide!

So, to finish: I'm going to Besançon!

My next job: to apply and fill out the forms (I'll keep the posts coming as and when developments occur!)

First Form Completed
NOVEMBER 25, 2015

This afternoon, I completed the Provisional Choices Form. This is the initial form you complete to tell the university what you want to do. I had to choose my preference by placing the number '1' (my first choice) next to the option I most wanted to do.

This form is handed to the person dealing with the year abroad and then, this will be reviewed and sent on to the university. If you're doing the Language Assistant job, the application is completed on line on the British Council website. However, the Provisional Choices Form still needs to be completed so that the university knows what you are doing. Also, it is a good idea to have a backup just in case the Language Assistant job falls through. If that happens, you have a Plan B to go to university as an Erasmus student.

I put my first choice as Besançon and my second choice as Aix-en-Provence.

I've handed this form in way before the deadline which is in January but this means now, if there are any issues, they will get back to me before it needs to be in. Also, it is one less thing to think about and I can tick it off the list of things to do.

Once the form is sent off, I should hear back from my chosen university and whether I have been accepted. If I have, the next stage will start and no doubt, there will be more forms and paperwork to be completed.

Résumé en français:

Cet après-midi, j'ai complété le formulaire de choix provisoire. C'est le premier formulaire qu'on doit compléter dans l'ordre à dire l'université ce que vous voulez faire. J'ai choisi par mettre '1' à côté de mon choix.

Ce formulaire doit être donné à la personne qui organise l'année à l'étrangère.

Si vous-voulez faire l'assistant de langue, vous pouvez remplir la demande en ligne: British Council (en anglais). Cependant, le formulaire devrait être complété parce que parfois, il y a des problèmes avec l'assistant de langue. S'il y a des problèmes, vous-pouvez toujours étudier en France comme un étudiant.

Mon premier choix est Besançon et mon deuxième choix est Aix.

Quick Update: Choix Confirmé
MARCH 4, 2016

It's been a little while since I have written a post, mainly because, well, there hasn't been much to say! But, I just received an email from my university which has confirmed my year abroad choice as Besançon. This means this will be sent to the university in France who, fingers crossed, will accept me and confirm my choice as definite. So, that's all, my choice has been allocated and I await the decision if I'll be accepted by Besançon.

Résumé en français:

Alors, je n'ai pas écrit un post depuis un moment parce que, franchement, je n'ai pas eu beaucoup à dire. Mais, je viens de recevoir un email de mon université qui a confirmé mon choix comme Besançon. Mon choix sera envoyé à l'université en France et, j'espère qu'elle m'acceptera. Donc, c'est tout. Mon choix a été envoyé et maintenant, je dois attendre pour la décision de l'université à Besançon.

Full Forms Ahead...
MARCH 10, 2016

So, after a period of not many things happening regarding my year abroad, last week I was sent an email confirming that I want to study in Besançon (L'université de Franche-Comté) . And, today, I had another year abroad meeting about the forms that I need to complete prior to going to France. The main and important forms are the Learning Agreement Form and the Erasmus Grant Form. I have attempted at completing both straight away to get the paperwork side of it out the way as soon as possible. Successfully, I have completed the Erasmus Form and sent it off to my university to be checked. This form is crucial because it is what releases the Erasmus money I need to help me live in France. The Learning Agreement Form is somewhat more complex and complicated and requires more time. I have made a start, filling in my personal details and other bits of information I know. Things like the modules I'll be choosing to study are not known yet and they are likely to change once I'm in France anyway. This form is much harder because it can't be completed all at once because some sections can only be filled in France or other sections have to wait until later in the year. But, getting the parts I can done now, helps a great deal so I can ask questions and any mistakes can be corrected.

Many of these forms are from the EU, making them sometimes a little harder to complete and complicated but I think getting them out the way sooner is better to avoid the stress of rushing them to reach the deadline.

So, to finish, that's two important forms completed – or partially, ready for the next stage which to be honest, I'm not sure what it will entail.

Résumé en français

Aujourd'hui j'ai assisté à une réunion sur les formulaires que je dois compléter avant d'aller en France. Les formulaires importants sont 'Learning Agreement Form' et 'Erasmus Grant Form'. Pour moi, c'est une bonne idée de finir les formulaires alors on n'a pas trop de formulaires! Heureusement, j'ai fini Erasmus Grant Form et je l'ai envoyé pour la vérification par mon université. "Erasmus money" ou l'argent d'Erasmus est essentiel parce qu'il me donnera l'argent que j'ai besoin de vivre en France.

Malheureusement, Learning Agreement Form est plus compliqué. J'ai complété mes coordonnées mais les autres choses je ne peux pas finir parce que je dois être en France.

Erasmus Codes: Where can I find them?
MARCH 16, 2016

While filling in the many forms for my year abroad, I kept coming across the term 'Eramsus Code'. I had never heard of it let alone know where to find them.

When I saw this box labelled Erasmus code, I was completely unsure what it meant or where I would get it from. I searched the Internet but I couldn't find much to help me. But after a little searching, I found this website which seemed to provide the answer: http://www.moveonnet.eu
Once you're on the website, click:

FOR STUDENTS
UNIVERSITY FINDER
SELECT THE COUNTRY YOUR UNIVERSITY IS IN
TYPE THE TOWN OR CITY IT IS IN
THE UNIVERSITY SHOULD BE FOUND
CLICK THE UNIVERSITY AND YOU WILL FIND ALL THE INFORMATION YOU NEED
INCLUDING ERASMUS CODES

In the know
APRIL 10, 2016

Recently, I was given the email address of a student who has just come back from Besançon.

This was a great opportunity for me to write and ask her about her time there and a get some advice so that I'm more in the know about my year abroad in Besançon.

I started by asking her a few basics such how to get to Besançon. She told me to take the Eurostar from London ST Pancras to Paris GARE du Nord and then go from Paris GARE de Lyon to Besançon VIOTTE.

I also asked her other questions on things I was unsure or worried about. One question I can remember asking about was what the rooms at the halls of residence were like and what was included in them.

I found this really useful to talk to someone who has been there and done it and I would recommend it if you are feeling overwhelmed or stressed by the whole thought of it.

So, my tip is, find out who has already completed their year abroad in the place you want to go to and ask questions…get in the know!

The Dossier
APRIL 13, 2016

I have just been told about something called 'The Dossier' which is a word document that has to be written while on the year abroad. The Year Abroad Dossier has to be 5000 words in total, 1000 words per section. There are four sections to write about:

Section 1: Evaluating Competence – which means evaluating your communication skills in the target language. See image below:

Section 2: identify your strengths and weaknesses, set your goals and targets for your year abroad. This section has to be written in the target language so, for me, this would be French.

Following Goals:

Language Acquisition – What aspects of language do you need to focus on?
Speaking (to friends or in more formal contexts)
Writing (letters, essays, emails etc.)
Listening (lectures, conversations, television etc.)
Reading (academic texts, newspapers etc.)
Grammar
Building vocabulary
Pronunciation
Register awareness

2. Cultural Competence – What cultural norms and values is it important to develop an understanding of?

Day to day social interaction (routines, eating and drinking habits, manners, dress codes)
Nonverbal communication (body language, facial expressions)
University life
the working environment
Socialising
Family life

3. Knowledge And Understanding – What aspects of the country's history, politics, cultural output, societal issues and/or economy do you need to find out more about?

4. Work-Related Skills – On which of the following work-related skills do you need to focus attention?

Communication
Problem solving
Information technology
Planning
Working with others

Decision-making
Meeting deadlines

Section 3: how you are going to achieve your goals?

Section 4: Evaluating Progress – Am I making progress in achieving the targets that I set myself at the beginning of my placement?

Year Abroad Scholarships
APRIL 21, 2016

A scholarship is something I'm not eligible for but, it may be worth you having a look if you are. They can be really useful and provide you with extra money to finance your year abroad. And, scholarships don't have to be paid back.

Of course, every university is different but check to see if your university offers any scholarships. For instance, my university, Nottingham Trent offers several.

NTU International Travel Scholarship

International Exchange Office Mobility Scholarship

Summer Mobility Scholarship

Santander Student Mobility Scholarship

I'll include a link to the Nottingham Trent scholarships page, which will give more information about the scholarships above. Although, this page is most useful for Nottingham Trent students, students from other universities may find it helpful and point them in the right direction to apply for a scholarship at their university.

Nottingham Trent Scholarships

Other useful websites:
http://www.thirdyearabroad.com/before-you-go/money-matters/item/1431.html
http://www.european-funding-guide.eu/scholarship/6526-erasmus-mundus-action-2-emp-aim

Trying to make head or tail of it
MAY 11, 2016

Today has been a day staring at a computer screen trying to work out and complete different documents. It's been a tad stressful to say the least (maybe this is what others meant when they spoke about French bureaucracy!)

First of all, the day started with me sitting down with my language assistant to change the modules I had chosen – mainly because some modules I had chosen could have been a bit of a waste of time because for instance, one module called 'La Grammaire et pratique de la langue anglaise' was about English grammar, particularly for French students. So, with a bit of adjusting and help from my assistant, we could find modules that suited and would benefit me better. It took a long time. I thought I'd be there for 20 minutes but it turned out to be 2 hours! I sent this is off to be checked and once they are confirmed, I will write a post about the modules I've selected.

Then, I thought I would ask her about applying for university accommodation because I wanted to know how and when to do it. Well, good job I did ask because we found out that I had missed the deadline to apply…yikes! So, again, with my assistant's help, she spoke to my other lecturer who made a call and found out that the deadline was in fact in 30th May (the page hadn't been updated) rather than 30th April…crisis averted for now! With some urgency, I thought it would be best if I get applying for accommodation. I clicked on 'comment obtenir le logement' (how to get accommodation) accommodation for Besançon thinking this is surely the best place to start but, I was probably a bit naïve over how it all works. On this page, there was just an email address and so I thought a quick email would do the trick. But no…later on I was told that I would need to apply for accommodation using this highly complex, French site. https://www.messervices.etudiant.gouv.fr/envole/portal/index.php#tab/1. Fortunately, if I hadn't had a French native sitting next to me to help, I think I would have pulled my cheveux out! It took a while to complete since it was full of acronyms and French admin jargon. Though, I got there in the end with a lot of help. I had to attach some pictures of proof of who I am – driving licence and student card. I felt relieved. I was advised to pick student accommodation in the city centre of Besançon because it is easier to get to my campus and it is around 300 euros a month – this would work out cheaper than getting the bus. I chose the following

Résidence Canot
Résidence Antide Janvier
Résidence Mégevand

http://www.crous-besancon.fr/logements/logement-crous/

After having struggled with this long application, I felt slightly less worried and under control of the situation. But, unfortunately, the good news doesn't last long. En route home from university, my phone buzzed and it was an email from mes services etudiant. They said my application had been refused because I hadn't demonstrated I was a student despite attaching a picture of my student card. They said, I would have to write a sworn statement in order for my application to be accepted. I did exactly that and sent it back off. I still haven't heard back from them so I don't know yet if my application has been successful and my preferences of where I want to live has gone through.As soon as I do, I'll write another post.

As you can see, it's been a little frustrating because you seem to get so far and then end up back at the beginning. Though, I can't complain because this is what the year abroad is partly, about, I'm not too worried about it. I couldn't expect the year abroad preparation to be all plain sailing.

Also, my lecturer has put me in contact with a student who is currently studying in Besançon but she is staying privately. This could be another option if the university CROUS accommodation doesn't work out because I could replace the girl currently living there which works out good for the landlord too because then there is always someone going to be there.

What's next now….well, I'm waiting to see if my application is accepted and my accommodation. It could be refused again because of the difficulty of confirming who I am. But, fingers crossed I'll have somewhere to live next year!

And finally, the application of mes services etudiants charges six euros to complete so I hope I don't have to reapply.

Thanks for reading this long, slightly moaning post…

#confused
MAY 11, 2016
This morning, I woke up to some emails from https://www.messervices.etudiant.gouv.fr/envole/portal/index.php#tab/1. They had sent me lots of

PDF documents which I need to print out and complete and send to them in the post to France in order to obtain accommodation. I'm slightly confused because I thought my application had been refused (see my post Trying to make head or tail of it). However, it looks like they have my accommodation choices and now I need to complete some paperwork within 8 days to secure a place to live. There is about 4 PDF files – all in French and asking for lots of things. I need to provide a photocopy of my passport, student card, my degree etc…. and also personal details. So, that's what I'll do now…

Keep you informed of what happens next!

It's a waiting game!
MAY 12, 2016

Following on from my last post #confused, I have printed out all the PDF files and completed them. The forms state that I need to send the following in the post to France:

Photocopy of my passport

Photocopy of my student card

Erasmus agreement from my university and my partner university (Nottingham Trent and Université de Franche-Comté)

Photocopy of my A level certificates

I haven't yet sent all this off, mainly because I need to check if what I have filled in is correct. And, I'm having a meeting with my year abroad tutor tomorrow. What's more, I need something called 'Lettre d'admission' from the university in France which I haven't got but the forms state I need. It is hard because I haven't yet completed any application to the university in France. Nottingham Trent have sent them my details, saying I want to attend the university but basically, it's a waiting game because I'm waiting for them to respond and send an email of how I can apply. Until then, I have no lettre d'admission (admission letter). I'm hoping that after my meeting tomorrow, I will be able to send all the forms to France because I have just eight days to get it to them. I'm also hoping that my university may be able to write their own lettre d'admission, which demonstrates that I am going to study in a French university establishment.

So, let's see how the meeting goes,

Until next time…

Résumé en français:

Donc, après avoir écrit mon dernier post #confused, j'ai imprimé tous les PDFs et je les ai complétés. Selon les formulaires, il faut envoyer:

Photocopie d'une pièce d'identité – mon passeport

Photocopie de ma carte d'étudiante

Photocopie du dernier diplôme obtenu

Un accord bilatéral – ERASMUS

Je n'ai pas envoyé ces formulaires en France parce que j'ai besoin de vérifier si j'ai complété correctement les formulaires. Je vais avoir une réunion avec mon prof demain. En outre, j'ai besoin d'obtenir une lettre d'admission de l'établissement en France que je n'ai pas.

C'est difficile parce que je n'ai pas complété une application à l'université française. Nottingham Trent a envoyé mon application à l'université en France mais je dois attendre pour un email.

Après la réunion demain, j'espère que je pourrai envoyer les formulaires en France parce qu'ils doit être renvoyés sous huit jours. Aussi, peut être mon université pourra écrire une lettre d'admission pour moi dans l'ordre pour prouver que je vais étudier dans un établissement en France.

Baby Steps
MAY 13, 2016

Today has been a really positive and proactive day. Shortly before my meeting with my year abroad tutor, I received an email saying that I would receive an email today with the application to Université de Franche-Comté. An hour or so later, I received an email stating I had been accepted "Nous aurons le plaisir de vous accueillir dans le cadre du programme d'échange Erasmus+ pour l'année universitaire 2016-2017." This means I am going to Besançon.

The email contained links to the application page which I have until the 17th June to complete. My previous application for accommodation will be cancelled and I will restart it. I also don't need une lettre d'admission as previously mentioned. And, if I do, I can use this email to confirm I have a place.

There was one slight problem, Nottingham Trent wasn't listed on the drop down list so, my year abroad tutor rang Besançon and they said, it will be fixed and ready for me to complete soon. Once I have done this, I will be able to apply for accommodation too.

So, I'm really happy with how this has gone. I have made huge progress in something which this time yesterday felt overwhelming. But, I've made baby steps today!

PS: the email states that I need to be in Besançon on the 1st September.

One small step for now, a giant leap for September
MAY 16, 2016

Following on from the previous post Baby Steps, I have completed my application to the university in France and I'll await further instructions.

On the form, it asked me to submit an image of my passport, my learning agreement forms, a form with the level of my French which was optional and other things relating to my personal details.

It was very straightforward and quick to do and all online which makes it easy. I don't know if I need to send anything off yet.

Faire Connaissance
MAY 24, 2016

I just had an email from the Université de Franche-Comté who informed me that I could join the buddy system and they will put me in touch with a local French student. The local buddy will be my first contact in Besançon and will able to help me to discover the city, help me to deal with administrative procedures such as at the bank etc.

I have made my request and I will wait to find who I am paired with.

See the links below for more information about the buddy system in Besançon.

http://esnbesancon.buddysystem.eu/

http://www.erasmus-besancon.com/

Erasmus Language Assessment
JUNE 2, 2016

I have just completed the online language assessment which assesses your grammar, vocab, listening, reading and writing in the language that you're studying.

It's all completed online and it's mandatory if you are to receive your Erasmus funding. The EU asks that it is completed before and after you go abroad to. The purpose of the assessments is to monitor how you have improved your language skills during the year abroad.

Your language is assessed using the CEFR framework (The Common European Framework of Reference for Languages) More information can be found on the link below and have a look at the video.

There are 4 levels:

A1, A2, B1, B2 ,C1, C2

https://europass.cedefop.europa.eu/en/resources/european-language-levels-cefr

Thank you and goodbye x
JUNE 12, 2016

This is my final post before I go to France and therefore, I want to take this opportunity to thank people who have made this all happen.

First of all, a thank you to my year abroad tutor and language assistant, who have helped me tackle the French admin and made calls to speed things along. I'm very grateful to you for your time and effort.

I'd like to say a huge thank you to my flatmates who have put up with my rambling, the many debates and my obsession with France. You have made second year an absolute joy. Thank you for the laughs and especially for the time and effort you put in making my last day memorable. We had a great time this year. I wish you only but success in all that comes your way. Have a wonderful summer break, enjoy the adventure and opportunities. Stay safe and best wishes to you all.

I'd like to say thank you to my family especially my mum, dad and stepdad for their unconditional love and support. I couldn't do without their wisdom and encouragement. Your support has come in all and many forms, and for that, I can't thank you enough. You have helped me get to where I am today and I always know that I can rely on you for advice. I'm sure my year abroad will bring challenges but, I know you'll be a call away. I love you xxx

To my girlfriend who has been my rock since I started university. Your encouragement, love, kindness and care has been priceless. You're my dearest friend. You have lended your ear, given your advice and made me laugh and smile. We have created fond memories together. We met in French and to think I am going to study in France 5 years later is incredible. Thank you Bella for everything, You are amazing. I couldn't wish for anything more for you than success and happiness in everything that comes your way. I love you Fiona xxx

Finally, to my Nan who passed away before I started university. Your love and bravery has been my guidance. I'll always be so proud of you. To you Nan, I hope you can see I've made it to France. I love you Nan xxx

It's been a blast, take care and thank you

Au plaisir – goodbye, see you soon

Matt

Don't forget to get the memo!
AUGUST 20, 2016

Today I was sent a link to complete the MEMO survey. This is a survey that has to be completed 14 days prior to leaving for your host country.

The survey has to be completed in order for the Erasmus money to be released once you arrive. So, don't forget to do it!

The survey consists of several questions relating to your personality. This helps to create an overall picture of you as a person; your strengths and weaknesses etc. This can be used to show employers.

The good thing about the MEMO survey is, it has to be completed again once you come back from the year abroad. This then shows you how the year abroad has changed and developed you as a person. For instance, the MEMO survey asks questions to help determine your confidence, social skills and adaptability. Once you get back, you can see how these things may have increased owing to the opportunities and experiences that the year abroad gives.

My 1st MEMO survey has definitely given me some areas I can focus on during my year abroad to improve.

Get memo-ing!

A la prochaine

Résumé en français

Aujourd'hui j'ai complété 'the Memo Survey'. Il faut de compléter le questionnaire 14 jours avant on va à l'étranger.

Le questionnaire doit être complété pour obtenir l'argent d'Erasmus. Donc, n'oubliez pas!

Il faut de répondre aux questions sur la personnalité qui aident à créer une image entière de soi.

Le questionnaire est utile parce qu'on doit le compléter avant et après être rentré. Donc, il permet à quelqu'un de voir leur développement.

Je peux utiliser le questionnaire pour concentrer sur les choses que j'ai besoin d'améliorer.

A la prochaine

DURING FRANCE

Arrivé!
AUGUST 29, 2016

So I've arrived in Besançon. Phew! It seems like only yesterday I was planning my year abroad but now I'm here.

I thought it would be a good idea to tell you about the journey.

I live not far from London so, I took the Eurostar from London St Pancras to Paris Gare du Nord. This was really simple for me as it was a bit like going door to door.

After arriving in Paris, Gare du Nord, I took a taxi to Gare de Lyon. This was really easy and convenient. I had a lot of luggage so the métro would have been stressful. The taxi costed around 14 euros.

Then, I had some lunch before getting the TGV train to Gare Besançon Viotte. The journey from Paris takes around 2 hours.

It was a really fun and easy way to travel. The train and stations are interesting and you get to see lots of beautiful parts of France along the way.

I highly recommend this way of getting here.

I am staying in the Ibis Centre Ville so that I can sort my university accommodation tomorrow. This hotel is ideal because it's located in the city centre so I can sort my university accommodation and do other things and have a base while I do it all.

I'll keep you updated as I'll have more to write no doubt in the next day or so!

1st day in Besançon
SEPTEMBER 5, 2016

So much has happened since arriving here that it's only now that I get the opportunity to write a post.

The 1st day in Besançon was hectic and dare I say, a little stressful. I woke up early to meet a girl who I had been partnered with as part of the buddy system the Université de Franche Comté has – see my post Faire Connaissance. We met at a bus stop not far from the hotel where I was staying and headed towards the university accommodation which is around 20 minutes by bus from the city centre. I bought a ticket for the day which costed 4 euros 30. I'd like to add that after being here now 5 days, the bus service is fantastic and really reliable. I have since bought a card which I renew every month to use on the buses and trams for just over 27 euros.

Once we arrived at the accommodation, we queued to collect my room keys. I wasn't surprised to find out that they didn't have any of the forms I had sent them and so, they weren't going to give me a room. However, this is where having a native person with you really helps. She explained to them that I was an Erasmus student and they eventually gave me a room key.

We took the bags to the room and I was pleasantly surprised. The rooms come with their own bathroom, fridge, desk and bed of course. It is a nice room and has a beautiful view of the hills.

After this, I wanted to head to the city centre to sort a bank account and mobile phone plan. We went to Credit Agricole https://www.credit-agricole.fr/ because this was advised by the university. I booked an appointment to see them to set up an account but, now I'm not sure if I do need a French bank account after all. If I do, I'll write a post about it. Instead, I have been using a currency card by Caxton https://www.caxtonfx.com/ and this has come in handy. You load the card with pound sterling and this converts to euros on the card to spend in shops and online. It works just like a normal debit card.

Then, we went to sort out a phone sim card. I wasn't sure if I could have one because I didn't have a French bank account to pay the phone bill but again, with the help of my buddy, we tried my British bank card because it was a Visa Debit card. And, it worked! The mobile plan I got is really good. I bought it from Free http://mobile.free.fr/ for 19 euros 99 a month and it comes with unlimited calls in France, unlimited calls to landlines in Europe, and unlimited messages in Europe and 50GB data. As well as, unlimited wi-fi in hotspots around the city.

After all of this, my buddy gave me a tour of the university and then we had lunch at the university restaurant which costs around 3 euros for a starter, main and dessert. You have 10 points and each dish is worth a point so a starter could be 3 points, main meal could be 6 and dessert could be 1 point. Something like that...still getting my head around it. But, it works very well. And you get, free bread and water. So, it's quite cheap to eat at lunch time.

My first day was tiring as I had to absorb a lot of information in French! But, we achieved a lot.

Erasmus Student Network
SEPTEMBER 9, 2016

Yesterday was quite a busy day again. At 10am I went to a meeting in the city centre, held the by the international relations office for Erasmus students.

It was a interesting meeting and reassured me that there is lots of help available if I need it.

I was given a bag full of leaflets and brochures to read and also a ticket to have a free meal in the canteen. I must say, it's really worth while eating in the university's restaurant as it's only 3€,25 for a starter, main and dessert + a bread roll.

After this, I had another meeting held by the Erasmus Student Network (ESN). The meeting felt a bit like a cross between an inspirational talk and a holiday rep meeting; there was music, videos, mascots, dancing etc. Nevertheless, this was just as informative.

The ESN Besançon team also provide help for Erasmus students but mainly they provide events and activists for us to do whilst in Besançon. They told us about trips to different parts of France – for example a trip to Strasbourg for €30. They also do free cinema, theatre and museum trips, food tasting events using produce from around the area Franche Comté. As well, tomorrow they are giving away free things for your room and kitchen utensils etc.

I bought an ESN card for 5€ because this gives you reductions and access to these events. Lots were free so even better!

After this, we had spokespeople from banks, associations, societies, drama and orchestra groups etc.

There are lots of things to get involved with and it felt like Erasmus students would be looked after well and experience different things whilst on the year abroad. What was nice, was the organisation of everything and the range of cultural and social events planned.

Donc à la prochaine!

Dossier inscription
SEPTEMBER 9, 2016

This morning I had a meeting (yes another!) held by the international relations office.

The purpose of this was to help us fill in our enrolment dossier (dossier inscription) . At the moment, I'm not officially enrolled at the uni, this is going to happen on Monday. Today's meeting, I just had to fill in lots of documents and booklets about myself for enrolment. The man said that even French people find all of this confusing so that's why we fill it in as a group!

After this, he told us the stuff we will need to bring to enrolment. Being in France and dealing with admin means one piece of paper won't do, you'll need to cut down a tree to make sure you have enough pieces of paper!

1) copie attestation (university confirmation letter)

2) 1 photo d'identité (picture of yourself)

3.) Photocopie de la carte d'identité (photocopy of passport or identity card)

4.) Photocopie de la carte medicale (photocopy of EHIC card)

5.) 1 enveloppe 50g (50g envelope)

6.) 1 enveloppe 20g (20g envelope)

I did my photocopying at the town hall for just 15 cents and bought the envelopes from the post office. Everywhere seems to have photocopiers (I think you have to photocopy your life in France!) so you'll bound to find one but the town hall is a good bet!

Le Jeu de Piste* and La Brocante*
SEPTEMBER 11, 2016

*Le Jeu de Piste = Treasure Hunt

*La Brocante = Bric-a-Brac

Yesterday was another beautiful day in Besançon and I spent the morning and afternoon in the city with other Erasmus students. The ESN (Erasmus Student Network) had organised an event where in small groups and a leader, we had to walk around the city, stopping at different spots and completing different activities such saying French tongue twisters as fast as possible, spelling out words using our bodies, dressing in fancy dress and having a picture taken, answering questions at La Maison de l'Europe about the EU, playing Pétanque , tasting the local cheese called Comté etc...

As well as this doing all this, I got to see a lot of the city and see where some of the museums are etc. Victor Hugo was from Besancon and the house where he lives has been converted to a museum. This looks an interesting place to go to soon.

It was a fun day and a good opportunity to meet more international Erasmus students.

After this, at 3pm there was La Brocante* at the Maison des Etudiants (student union). La Brocante means Bric-a-Brac and so, there was a room full of items such as microwaves, pots, glasses, pans, cutlery, hobs, etc......the list goes on! You could take for free anything you wanted. The items were donated by past students who had maybe left things behind or given to the ESN to give to new students. You were given 30 credits to make it fair in order to stop people from taking all the most expensive items. Pots and pans and small kitchen items were around 2 credits but microwaves and big kitchen appliances and toasters were 30 credits so you couldn't take anymore items once you had used all the 30 credits. This was a great idea and enabled you to pick up for free stuff you hadn't got or forgotten to get.

Au coiffeur et à la piscine
SEPTEMBER 21, 2016

Salut à tous/toutes

I thought I'd give you an update of la vie en France! Yesterday, I went to all the places in a town that you learn in a year 5 French lesson – le coiffeur (the hairdressers) and la piscine (the swimming pool)! I've been in France 3 weeks today and so, my hair needed a trim – those who know me know that I like to keep it short! But also, I really wanted to confront my fear of going to a French hairdressers and so, I thought I should get it done as soon as I could. I wasn't afraid of the actual haircut, just the thought of knowing what to say etc. But anyways, there are lots of barbers in Besancon and so I chose one and went in. As I went in, the lady asked if I had an appointment and I said no, but there wasn't a problem, she said I could be seen now. She put me in a chair and then before I knew it, my hair was being washed and shampooed and massaged! I thought maybe I had chosen a high-end kind of place! After that, this was the bit I feared the most. She took me to the chair and asked what I wanted. I explained, short on the sides, trim on top. And well, to cut a long story short (no pun intended), she understood and I got exactly what I had wanted. It felt just like England. So, what was I so worried about?! The lady was really nice too, and asked me lots of questions, checked I was okay throughout etc. It was a really nice experience and I wonder now why I was dreading it so much. It was fine and I was pleased and slightly proud of myself for doing it. I had envisioned myself growing long hair because I was too scared to get it cut! It all came to 16 euros which is quite good considering the wash and shampoo and the nice atmosphere etc. I definitely know where I can get my haircut now which makes you feel more settled.

Next challenge of the day was going swimming. I had a coupon for free entry to a swimming pool, just outside the city centre. I took the tram to Allende which was about 15 minutes by tram but there is a bus too. I really enjoy swimming so I thought this would be a good thing to do. I headed to the swimming pool and well, that was fine too. French swimming pools are quite hot on hygiene – you have to wear a swimming hat and to get into the changing rooms, you have to take your shoes off, walk through a shower that washes your feet, get changed, get showered with soap, pass through another shower and then enter the pool! It was good fun and I hope to keep the swimming up. I swam for about an hour before heading back to university for the afternoon.

Voilà c'est tout! Hope everything is going well wherever and whatever you're doing,

A plus!

Modules
SEPTEMBER 26, 2016

Bonjour à tous/toutes

I know it's another day and another blog post…sorry! I've got to keep the fans happy!

This time, I thought I'd write about the modules I'm doing at university. They took some time to sort out and a bit of tweaking but I, or rather we (my coordinator) got there in the end.

In the UK, as you're probably aware, we have to get 120 credits to pass the year – 60 credits for semester 1 and 60 credits for semester 2. In France and I think across Europe, they work on a different system and so, use European credits. To pass the year in France, you need 60 European credits – 30 for each semester.

Most modules in France are worth 6 European credits, meaning I have to do 5 modules per semester. However, some are worth less – 2/3 European credits so that means you have to do more modules to make 30 credits.

There is a mixture of French lessons for international students – français perfectionnement and français échanges internationals and then, translation classes, translating texts from French towards English and then English towards French. The module called La Culture Anglophone is about British artwork and is really interesting, analysing the paintings etc. This is taught in English. Technique d'expression en langue française is a really useful module and is about teaching French natives how to improve their written French. French is actually quite challenging grammatically – many different rules etc and so, lots of French people struggle with this. I was told by many lecturers that French students spell words how they sound or they forget certain agreement rules etc…I won't get too complex! Anyways, it is very useful and actually reassures you that if French people make mistakes, I shouldn't be too hard on myself when I do.

Also, to clarify why it says 32 credits in total despite what I said above. Basically, I'm allowed to do more than 30 credits – the excuse because I am an Erasmus student and also, if I do badly in one exam, I can get rid of it at the end.

So, that's it…hope it helps. I'll keep you updated all being well.

Bonne semaine et à plus!

Update from across the Channel
OCTOBER 25, 2016

Hello again,

I thought I'd do an update of life here again as I prepare to start half-term at the end of this week.

I have just had a look and can't believe that I have been writing this blog for nearly a year. My first post was published on the 28th October 2015. Wow, that year has gone quick. Despite all the prep and the inevitability of coming on a year abroad, I still can't imagine that a year ago I was preparing to come here and now a year later, I'm in Besançon. It's scary to say the least how the time goes.

Not only that, how settled I feel in this country. I mean, don't get me wrong, I miss home and the familiarity of it and of course my friends and family but, France has become strangely more normal for me now. Of course, I hate to write this and assume everything is great because, this is just today's feeling. Tomorrow, I could be crying out for home! But I suppose the essence of what I am saying and what the year abroad is about, is to live in the present moment and learn to forget about what happened yesterday, maybe the blunders and try not to predict the future. I hope I take this way of thinking home with me. Anyways, enough of the deepness and more to an update of life here! I can hear my friends and family smiling or yawning, knowing that I was always go off topic and will spend some hours talking deeply about these things. So, sorry. Not much changes I'm afraid.

Being me, I do like to provide a weather update. It's been rather grey these last few days and cloudy. Not too cold. It doesn't ruin anything because sometimes the weather is just perfect for the situation.

Last week, it was a busy uni week as usual. I had several exams to do which seemed to go okay. At the weekend, I went to a market in Besançon which had stalls selling gifts and food from different parts of France and Europe. Sunday, I did my weekly swim.

Monday, I had my 2 hour lecture and then I went to a shopping centre, Chateaufarine which is brilliant. It has everything you need. My mouse on my laptop has been playing up and I couldn't find a cat to sort it so I thought I'd get a new USB plug-in mouse from a technology shop called Boulanger.

Tomorrow I have a long day again but then Thursday, all being well, I start my half-term. I am fortunate to have my family come out to see me so I hope they are brought safely here.

That's all I suppose for now. I hope this finds you well wherever you are.

With all my wishes from Besançon,

Au plaisir,

Matt

Bank or no bank?
OCTOBER 27, 2016

I just quickly wanted to share my advice on financing your year abroad because I've been asked by a few people about this. Before arriving, I was sure that I would need to open a French bank account. However, I haven't needed to because I have a currency card. This works just like a debit card and you load money from a UK bank account onto it and it converts it into Euros or whatever currency you set it to. This means, I can use it without being charged like I would if I were to use a UK bank card.

There are several currency cards to use, I suggest you have a look on-line but I use Caxton and this was recommended on Third Year Abroad.com. It is really useful and so, I would say, get a currency card and you won't need to open a bank account when you arrive. Though, if you decide to work, I would imagine you would need a bank account for your employer to pay your wages into. But, do check. If you're studying, the currency card is the perfect solution.

"If you don't climb the mountain, you can't see the view!"
OCTOBER 31, 2016

This weekend, I was fortunate enough to have my family come and visit me. I had a great time showing them around Besançon. On the Saturday, we took the bus up to La Citadelle, which is a world heritage site, steeped in history. It was occupied by the Germans in the Second World War and as a place, has witnessed some of the cruelest things humans can do. It is a fascinating but sombre place.

I visited the Citadelle when I first arrived in Besançon but I wasn't bored because you can never get over the view of Besançon from the top. And, like last time, we had great weather which meant we could see for miles across Besançon. It takes your breath away being so high up and looking down on the world.

Day Out in Ornans
OCTOBER 31, 2016

Today, I took a coach from Besançon to Ornans. Ornans is a typical Franche-Comté village and was the birth place of Gustave Courbet, a famous impressionist artist. Much of Courbet's work was of Ornans. The painting below was one he did of Ornans.

The coach took around 45 minutes to get to Ornans from Besançon and the journey was incredible. The view of the Franc-Comtois countryside and the mountains was stunning.

Also, the coach cost only 6 euros return which was really good. One downside, it only came every 3 hours. But, I spent a lot of time in the Courbet museum, looking at his artwork and taking pictures of the village.

Ornans was a beautiful village and I took lots of photos of the place. I can see what Courbet loved painting this town and area.

Vrai ou faux, the French like to strike?
NOVEMBER 21, 2016

There are many stereotypes that exist about the French and indeed France but, how many are actually true? I thought that, maybe, I could do a post a week about which stereotypes are true and which are false. So, there's no better place to start than the question, do French people like to strike?

Before coming on my year abroad, I learnt a lot about France's history especially, this aspect of protesting and striking. I was taught of course about the French Revolution which is where maybe, France's love with rioting and protesting started. Last year, I was taught about May 68 which was a student riot which took place across France, notably in Paris. These students were deeply angered by the overcrowding and poor conditions of their universities but also, the social changes which were happening in France spurred them to revolt against the status quo. So, I knew France had a long history and reputation for rioting and protesting but then, I didn't know how much of it still happens today. Can students still feel the need to protest, it's not like we are still in 1968?

Well, I can safely say, nothing much has changed since 1968. In 2016, French students still protest and it's not just students. The French do like to strike or display their disagreement with near about anything.

I would say, at least weekly, I am handed a sheet of paper as I enter university, urging students to se mobiliser and lutter – mobilise and fight! Today, it was no different. Another Monday morning, brings another topic to protest about. The university is planning to axe certain degree subjects owing to finance problems. Tomorrow, there is a meeting happening to protest about this and try to get students to stop it happening! I've attached a picture of the piece of paper I was given. I find it so interesting to read them and the use of language they use. French students are really very passionate about protesting and use words that demonstrate a fight for justice!

'Etudiant.e.s, nous n'avons d'autre choix que de nous mobiliser massivement pour s'opposer à ces mesures et éviter un désatre!
Students, we have no other choice but to get ourselves together and oppose these measures and avoid a disaster!'

So, yes, it's true, French people, especially students, like to strike, protest, revolt, whatever you want to call it. This is by far, a stereotype that we have got right...

France's Security
NOVEMBER 21, 2016

Bonjour à tous/toutes,
I thought I'd write a little about France's security because I think it's important that I write posts that reflect daily life in France instead of just the pretty side of France.

I didn't think it would be of honest of me to constantly post pictures of a perfect France because this doesn't necessarily show the truth. This country is still under a state of emergency which is blindingly obvious especially in large cities. There is strong military presence and the image above shows some armed soldiers patrolling the streets of Besançon.

France has been the target for several terrorist attacks this year and it is approaching a year since Paris was victim to the worst attack ever seen, killing 130 people on the 13th November 2015.

As a non-native, I feel the threat and fear that exists in France. I adore France and I have been able to visit some beautiful places but, this shouldn't detract or make an illusion to the fact that France is still reeling from terrorism. The presence of the army is reassuring but only strengthens the impression that France is prepared for the next attack on its soil.

Sorry to write a sombre post, but I did want to write an honest personal view of life in France. It would not be fair or realistic to only show the good side of a country which is currently dealing with many social problems.

Mulhouse Trip
NOVEMBER 28, 2016

Bonjour à tous et toutes,

This weekend I went to a Christmas market in Mulhouse, a city very close to the German and Swiss border.

I took the local train to Besançon TGV train station and then took the TGV train straight to Mulhouse. It took about an hour. The train was actually going to Strasbourg which is another place I really want to go to.

I had a great day looking around the market and I tried some regional food such as a potato, cheese and bacon dish and also hot wine and hot orange juice with honey, which kept me warm.

Mulhouse was so different to Besançon, so it was interesting to get out of my region and explore other parts of France. The German influence on the city was really evident too, in fact, it felt more German than French. The street signs were in German and French and I saw many cars with Swiss and German number plates.

Sorting out Semester 2
DECEMBER 7, 2016

Good morning everyone,

This is my last week in France before, all being well, I return to England next week. It's been a whirlwind couple of months here and so much has happened since September. It is always strange to think that when I arrived, it was really hot, temperatures reaching nearly 35 degrees, but now it is barely reaching 1 degree outside! It just shows how things have changed.

The last two weeks have been dominated by exams, I hope to write about this later on in the week when my exam on Friday is finished.

Anyway, since this semester is coming to a close, I wanted to meet with my coordinatrice to talk about semester 2 and the lessons I can do when I come back to France after Christmas. I would like to say, my coordinatrice has been so helpful and sorted many things out for me. Yesterday, I met with her to organise and plan semester 2. The meeting went really well and I now have a timetable for semester 2 and I know the lessons I can go to. No doubt however, it might need changing slightly when I get back but at least it is something to go on.

Hope everything is well with you. Thanks for your loyalty in reading.

Matt

Exams done!
DECEMBER 9, 2016

I've just finished my last exam for this semester. I had an exam for every subject I did so around 11. Over the last few weeks, I have had around 1 or 2 exams a week. Though, owing to a strike last week, my exams were moved around and rescheduled for this week because they couldn't happen on the strike days.

Just a bit of information about the exams:

Some exams took place in the classroom others, were in lecture theatres.
Since I take a lot of translation modules, the majority of my exams involved me translating either French towards English or English towards French. I have to say, I prefer French – English because I feel you can make the translation your own and express yourself freely, which makes sense when English is your native language!
The exam style is very different to what happens in the UK. Students arrive late and they are still accepted in. Also, bags are sometimes put at the front of the room and sometimes you can keep them next to you. You are asked to turn phones off but they are not taken from you.
Generally, the exams last around 1 -2 hours but you can leave whenever you finish. Some students left after 20 minutes or so. It feels very relaxed overall.
This semester has gone really well and I look forward to returning to start my new modules, all being well, in 2017! I do hope to write one last time before I go back to England on Monday.

Home Bound for Blighty (and a thank you)
DECEMBER 12, 2016

Good morning,

I'm sat on the TGV at Besançon ready to leave for Paris. It's was an early start as the train leaves at 6:39am as this is one of the only direct trains to Paris from here. The other TGV trains you need to change at the Besançon TGV station.

I arrive at Paris Gare de Lyon just after 9am and then I need to get the metro or bus to Gare du Nord to catch the Eurostar to London St Pancras.

Finally, I just want to say a huge thank you to my family, my girlfriend and my friends for their support and guidance. Without any of them, my first term here would have been so much harder. Thank you for your unconditional love to me. It's been a crazy 4 months but I did it thanks to you.

Have a great Christmas break and I hope to bring you some more posts in 2017.

Alors, allons-y!

Matt x

Back for Round 2
JANUARY 8, 2017

This is my first post in 2017 so, Happy New Year! I arrived back in a snowy Besançon yesterday evening after spending 3 weeks at home for Christmas. Where did the time go?!

I had a great time being back with my family and girlfriend after being away from them since September so a massive thank you for making my Christmas break special.

To be honest, it feels very strange to be in France again after almost forgetting all about university and life in Besançon. Whilst being home, it felt as if I hadn't ever even gone to France. I slipped straight back into British life which I didn't realise I missed until I was home.

Besançon and England are so different that although it takes the time to readjust, it also makes settling in easier because the two worlds don't meet, enabling you to separate them and in some ways, lead a double life.

Anyways, I'm back now to face semester 2. I have sorted my timetable and I start my new modules on Tuesday.

A la prochaine fois!

The love-hate relationship
JANUARY 9, 2017

I think anyone who studies a foreign language experiences a love-hate relationship with it. Some days, you can't get enough of it. Other days however, the very thought of it brings you out in a cold sweat. Well, that's what I have found whilst living in France.

There are days when I understand everything, speak about anything and these are the times that I love French. Then, there are days when I feel so English that I make mistakes in French and struggle to understand what someone is saying. These are the moments when I hate French and just want to fall back on my native language.

Therefore, the opportunity to study and live in France has done me a world of good for many reasons but mainly, it has shown me that learning a language is like being in a relationship. There are highs and lows and of course, I never actually hate French, it just there are times when you don't get on with it as best as you could. But I don't think this is abnormal, I think it makes French a 'living' experience which is interesting. It brings with it some challenges but also, some highly rewarding moments when you learn new words, new phrases, new ways of speaking. As native speakers, our language and how we converse with others forms a big part of our identity and it is hard to reconstruct this once you have developed your maternal language. However, learning a foreign language enables you to play with language, say different things and experiment. That is something I have learnt to do in France, experiment with language in order to build upon my identity.

Also, being at home for three weeks has allowed me to reflect a little on my 4 months in France and

26

take stock of French as a language. I think I became so bogged down in making sure I don't make any mistakes that French seemed a harder relationship that it ought to be. However, whilst at home and having a break from French, I was able to think about all that I have learnt and achieved in French over the last few months, I didn't choose to do this, I think being away from something allows you the time to gather your breath and sit back for a moment. The months before Christmas were so hectic that this pause never really took place and so, you never had the chance to assess where you have come. I certainly feel that the break from French that I had, has given me more confidence to experiment with the language and not get so worried about whether I make mistakes. I have become more relaxed with it which makes helps you because when you are more relaxed, you will sound more natural in the way you speak. What's more, being home reminds you of who you are and where you come from. I am English and what I was lacking prior to coming to France, was identity. I feel that France has made me proud to be English because this is one of the things you can come back to when home and family feel distant in your heart. I was scared making a mistake in French would reveal my Englishness but now, I am proud to show my nationality through the way I speak.

Therefore, being absent from home has taught me to appreciate the Englishness in me and where I come from.

First week of Uni
JANUARY 13, 2017

It's Friday evening and the snow has been falling on/off all day here in Besançon. So, since it's pretty snowy outside and rather cosy in my room, I thought it would be a good time to look back on my week at university. I'm not sure if it's because I enjoy the lessons more or because I am more settled in this time around, but I have really enjoyed my first week back. It has been interesting and I am happy with the modules I have chosen. There is a slight timetable problem that I need to sort out but apart from that, the lectures and the work have made me eager to learn more.

I started university on Tuesday with a module taught by an English man who taught me last semester. I enjoyed his lessons last time and so, I wanted to carry on with his module this term. This module is called expression d'entreprise (learning to express yourself in a Business context). So far, we have looked at how to write emails and letters in English and French. Of course, I know how to do the English part but refreshing yourself on the format of both languages is useful. For instance, French letters put the recipient and sender address on the opposite send to an English letter and also, French letters will include the city/town with the date for example: Besançon le 13 janvier.

After this lesson, I had translation from English to French with a French man, who I don't know but seems nice. We looked at a novel which was in English and needed to be written in French.

Later on in the day, I had French for Erasmus students. It is taught by a French lady who taught me the same subject last semester. I enjoy these lessons because we do some French grammar and also we read news articles and discuss them. It is a very good lesson for Erasmus students. I would say, it is similar to a French lesson at school but rather more intense and harder (of course).

Wednesday, I started at 8 am and it was analysing films with another French woman. This course is a mixture of French and English. The woman speaks both a little English and French depending on how difficult the thing she is saying may be. The other students are all French and so, Erasmus students are a minority. I like it though because you can be immersed into a French lecture and the teacher will speak at a speed designed for French natives. Although this is hard, it is also very good for your listening skills. I do like it though when she returns to English just to make sure I have understood what she said. I love films and analysing them so I have felt that this module suits me. I have always had a passion for film studies after having taken the subject at GCSE.

Next, I have a subject called Traductologie with an English man. This subject doesn't involve any translating, it is more the theory of translating. This is also really fascinating and I enjoy it a lot. The module is taught in English. For instance, this week we looked at the reasons why some translations are word for word translations. For example, sometimes, you cannot get away from translating a text word to word from French to English. However, there are other times when you need to change the whole text completely to make it make sense for the reader.

The other subject I do after this, is one I find very beneficial. I took it last semester and it is taught all in French. This is a module that helps to improve both your written and spoken communication in French. It is aimed for French natives who need to help with expressing themselves in French. We do French grammar, word of the day – to increase our vocabulary etc. We also do presentations in French about society and different forms of communication. I highly recommend this module because it is for French students and so despite being the only foreign student in the classroom, I feel that I have a rich opportunity to see how French is taught to natives and the difficulties they face.

On a Thursday, I do a lot of translation modules including one with a French woman who moved to the English-speaking part of Canada when she was young. She has now moved back to France and said that she is training herself to re-speak French after being in an English-speaking environment all her life. She said how she reads and speaks English daily and thinks in English so coming back to France has been a challenge but enables her to see the problems we will have as translators when you think in one language but have to translate into another. I find her and the lesson incredibly interesting and she made me feel very passionate for translation. She is a lovely woman too and I liked her approach to teaching. As Canada is a bilingual country, French and English are spoken and used everywhere. Some parts, however, like the Quebec area of Canada is nearly all French-speaking. Since she has lived in Canada, she said that as a translator, you have to be aware of the cultural elements that will affect your translation. Here is an example, in France, the French quite like using English words. Weekend in French is le week-end and le parking is a car park. However, in Canada they have their own French and like to stick to French rather than using English words. She told us that in Canada, they say *la fin de la semaine* (the end of the week). For French people and English people, if we say *the end of the week*, it means Friday. However, *la fin de la semaine* in Canadian French means the weekend – Saturday and Sunday. Therefore, as a translator, you have to be aware of these cultural differences. Her life in Canada brings a lot to the lesson and I look forward to working with her.

That's all. I am hoping that nothing changes too much with my new timetable but we are in France after all so anything can happen!

Hope all is well for you wherever you are,

Bon week-end

Stereotype check-up: Are the French rude?
JANUARY 22, 2017

I have been meaning to do more posts about French stereotypes after saying I would write about a different stereotype every week. Well, it didn't quite happen so....sorry! However, here is a stereotype of the French I would like to write about – Are the French rude? In England, we have a view that the French are impolite people and although I cannot generalise this whole nation, I can safely say, I have found the contrary to this stereotype.

So, are the French rude? No, is the answer. There are some rude French people (of course) like there are rude English people but generally what I have found is, they are very polite people. I would say, I come across more ill-mannered folk in the UK than I do in France.

What makes them polite? There are several key things that make the French people seem more polite than the English. The first is, they say 'Bonjour' all the time even if you don't know them. I have been in a cafe eating and not only will the staff say 'Bonjour' but also the customers. Likewise, in the hairdressers, as soon as someone walks in, the customers and the staff say 'Bonjour Madame' or 'Bonjour Monsieur'.

The second form of politeness, the French will kiss or shake hands with everyone they know, followed by 'ça va?' Also, when they leave each other, they will do the same thing. At the end of a lesson, they will kiss or shake hands with their friends who maybe they didn't see during the lesson etc.

Third thing, they will say 'Bon appétit' (enjoy your meal) when you eat. It only happened once, but I was eating in a cafe and a man was eating his lunch also said bon appétit to me.

Forth experience, when you want to talk to someone, be it your teacher, a shop assistant, they tend to say, 'dites-moi' or 'j'écoute' which translates as 'tell me/let me know' or 'I'm listening'. Of course in England, we do say, how can I help but I feel that these phrases in French are more polite because of the sense that the put emphasis on wanting to listen to you.

'Madame', 'Monsieur' – 'sir' or 'madam' is used by everyone in France. As soon as they say hello, they will probably address you with 'madame' or 'monsieur.' They have respect for each other, which is how it feels to me.

The fifth form of politeness, they like to help you. French people seem to really enjoy offering help to you when you're either lost, having language issues, or you need some assistance in a shop. I have experienced all three things and they seem to jump at the opportunity to help. I walked into a shop and I was looking for some jeans and shoes. I asked for some shoes similar to what I was wearing. I was shown where they wear. Then, I was looking at some jeans, the man came up to me and said, those jeans over there would go better with those shoes. I didn't ask for any fashion help but he gave it so, that I made the right purchase. Another similar example is that I picked up a jumper in size small because it looked quite big in the medium. I took it to the till and the man said, I think you should get the medium because it might be too tight in the small. He was right. I was so pleased he told me because the medium is a perfect size. Also, they love you to speak French, even if you just give it a try. The French seem to love helping you to get it right or correcting you. It is never done in a cruel way, you can tell that they like to correct your mistakes so that you improve. If you get it wrong, they don't care, they are friendly and make you feel less intimidated or embarrassed.

I can by no means generalise or say this is true throughout France, but this is what I have personally found during my time in Besançon.

Flying the Flag
JANUARY 28, 2017

Since the French are a patriotic bunch, it's no surprise that the French tricolour can be seen flying in a variety of places. From the town hall to the train station, the French flag is a common sighting wherever you go and shows that it still has the respect that it deserves in modern French life.

This is one stark difference between the UK and France. Although we might see the Union Jack being flown from the rooftops of governmental buildings in London or crowds might wave it when they wait outside Buckingham Palace, the Union Jack is very rarely displayed with so much honour. I think as British people, we can easily discuss the reasons why our flag doesn't seem to command the same patriotism, often the Union Jack has negative connotations, associated more with the extreme-right. The Union Jack has been shamed by nationalist groups whereas, in France, this hasn't happened. To fly the French flag only provokes sentimental feelings towards France and its values of liberty, equality and fraternity.

We see the very same ideology in other countries, particularly in the U.S where homeowners will fly the U.S flag outside their homes. France isn't quite this patriotic but nevertheless, it is prouder of its flag than we are in the UK which I hope will change.

Money Matters: budget, budget, budget
JANUARY 30, 2017

Budgeting sounds like common sense, not only for students living abroad but for anyone at university. And, you're right. Budgeting is important whatever you're doing but, I think learning to budget and manage your money is even more crucial when you're living in another country. I'll explain why…

You might think that budgeting on a year abroad is less of a worry since you will have student finance and Erasmus money. This is true but, with this extra money, comes a need to use it responsibly. You will receive ALL your Erasmus money in your account. It is not paid to you every few months. This sounds amazing and it is, but there is a temptation to spend it as soon as you get it. Work out all your outgoings and then, you can use the Erasmus money to possibly pay your bills. Anything left over is yours to use for whatever you want. Also, with your student finance money, you could make sure all your bills are paid for and then once again, anything left over is yours to keep. So, bills sorted, you can combine your Erasmus money and student finance money to make sure you can have fun.

Living in your home country doesn't come with the same stress as studying abroad. Your home country is your safety net, you have friends and family at your disposal much more easily. However, when you go abroad, the safety of your home to fall back on has gone. This means stress and homesickness can get to you. Then, if you add money problems, you could be adding insult to injury. So, managing your money and budgeting will keep your life less stressful.

Another point, the year abroad can sometimes demand more money. For instance, most of us have phone contracts and these still need to be paid for when we are abroad. If you use it, there is a high likelihood that you will be charged extra because of data roaming. This is something that needs to be budgeted for. Or, are you going to get a local sim card? If so, this will mean that you have two costs to cover – your home contract and a foreign phone contract. This needs to be budgeted for.

Of course, there are obvious outgoings such as rent that needs to be budgeted for but don't forget transport – will you need a bus pass that has to be renewed monthly?

Anyways, sorry to bring you a father kind of money lecture. Having said that, I couldn't have done without my dad to help me with a budget. If you have an iPhone, the app store has some good budgeting and money apps to keep you on track – check them out.

Find your 'exutoire': beat the stress
JANUARY 30, 2017

The year abroad can, without a doubt, cause you to feel stressed and overwhelmed. There are too many reasons to mention as to why you may experience stress while you are abroad.

Speaking from experience, I have certainly had moments of stress during my time in France especially at the beginning of the year abroad where there seems to be so much to do and sort out in such a short period of time. But also, stress can pop up throughout the year as you experience different challenging situations. That's why I advise anyone who feels stressed during their year abroad to take up a hobby.

The word I mentioned in the title, 'exutoire' means outlet or release in French and is used to describe something you do to release your stress. For me, I decided to take up swimming. I saw a swimming pool en route home once from university so, I thought it would be a good way to exercise, keep fit and keep any stresses at bay. Not only that, I thought it would be another way to experience another part of French society and practise speaking French in a new context other than at university and in the shops.

I'm really pleased I did this because when I leave the swimming pool, I feel refreshed and my mind is clearer. Of course, if you're not sporty, it doesn't matter, you can do anything you like as long as it makes you feel better and keeps your mind and body healthy. Just to make it clear, I don't encourage drinking a whole bottle of wine to drown out your sorrows! Do something that will leave you feeling good rather than a hangover. If you live somewhere pretty, go for a walk, take in the views, go to the cinema, meet some friends etc. Whatever you do, keep safe and healthy and hopefully, any stresses or worries you have will soon go away.

So, all there is left to say is, your exutoire is waiting for you, go get it!

Train of Thought
FEBRUARY 1, 2017

I was having a think about what post to write about next and then I realised that I haven't spoken about the transport here in Besançon and how I tend to get around. So, here's your transport guide!

To get to university:

Bus Company: GINKO

Monthly bus pass: 28 euros (as of 2017) – covers the whole GINKO bus network including trams.

If you live on campus, take line 3 in the direction of Rivotte via the train station. Get off at Republique.

Getting around Besançon

The bus network is quite big for a small city. Use the GINKO website to find the bus network lines and routes. There are trams from the city centre to the train station and to the suburbs. The trams take you around most of the key parts of Besançon. You can use your GINKO pass to travel on these.

To get back to campus:

Take line 3 from La Poste or Courbet in the direction of Temis via the train station.

To get to Arc-et-Senans (see my pictures to learn more)

Train Company: SNCF

From Besançon Gare SNCF to Arc-et-Senans

Take the TER (Train Express Regional – local train) direct to Arc-et-Senans. The cost varies but you can buy a fairly cheap ticket. The journey takes around 20-25 minutes.

To get to Dijon:

Train Company: SNCF

From Besançon Gare SNCF to Dijon

Take the TER direct to Dijon. Cost varies but can be cheap if booked in advance.
Use http://www.sncf.com/ to book tickets.

To get to Ornans (see my pictures to learn more)

Coach: Line A from Besancon Gare SNCF to Ornans. The coach stop is outside the train station. See the links below to help you get there.

http://www.ornans-loue-lison.com/fileadmin/user_upload/sommaires/VIE_PRATIQUE/besancon_pontarlier_via_ornans.pdf

http://www.ornans-loue-lison.com/vie-pratique/venir-et-se-deplacer.html

Mulhouse

Train Company: SNCF

Train: TGV (Train Grande à Vitesse) – high-speed train

Book in advance on the SNCF website.

From Besançon Gare SNCF direct to Mulhouse station.

Dole (see pictures)

Train Company: SNCF

TER from Besançon Gare SNCF to Dole

Local train so quite cheap.

If you want to find out about more great places to visit in the Franche-Comté region, have a look at the regional tourist website: http://www.franche-comte.org/

Are we a spoon-feed nation?
FEBRUARY 2, 2017

Following on from my other posts about the stark differences between the UK and France, I wanted to talk about the communication or rather the lack of it that exists here at my university in France.

When I talk about communication, I am talking about the way teachers and the university make sure students are aware of what is happening.

In the UK, well at least at my university, we seem to be told about everything via email. If a teacher is absent, going to be late, room change etc, we are kept informed. To me, this was normal and in some ways, expected. Of course, it is expected to be told these things, right?

Fast forward to France and, I ask this question, are we a spoon-feed nation back at home? I can say, from my experience here, France doesn't do communication. If a teacher is absent, it's up to you to check your timetable before coming to a lesson to find out, the same for a room change. And even, when my exams were moved about because of the strikes, was I informed of this? You guessed, no. They see it as your responsibility to know what is happening and not the teacher's job to send out emails telling you about changes to a class. There have been some instances when I have turned up at a lesson to find that the teacher is not in and I thought, I was never told. It is funny too, it seems to be the only English natives that turn up and the other nationalities don't – I presume that they are in the habit of checking their timetable before leaving home. Whereas for us British people, we assume that we will be told. This is a wrong assumption to make and so, I have learnt to check and recheck throughout the day if the lesson is in the same place, same time and the teacher will be there.

I am by no means wanting to criticise the system here because I generally feel it works very well. However, there are some differences that require time to get used to.

These communication differences should not be labelled good or bad, they are simply, just that, differences. Britain likes to keep us updated, France likes you to do it yourself – it depends on what suits you best. I would say, I do think France is lacking and could be better at keeping us informed of major changes that are happening. But I don't think they are in any rush to do so…

Bonne Soirée!

Back into the swing of things
FEBRUARY 8, 2017

Despite being back in France only a month, mid-semester exams and assessments are already starting…they don't wait around that's for sure!

I was more or less thrown into the deep end as my first assessment of the year took place today. For a first assessment, it was rather a nerve-wracking experience as I had to speak for five minutes in French in front of French native students about a book I had read. I chose to speak about two books that I bought last year called Mon Bataclan and Je suis Paris which are about the terrorist attacks in Paris in November 2015. Mon Bataclan is, in fact, a comic strip written and drawn by a victim of the attack in the Bataclan theatre which was stormed by terrorists during a concert there. Je suis Paris is an incredible book that contains 7,709 letters and notes left by people at the places where attacks happened. There are some beautiful, moving and sad letters to victims and their families written by anonymous people, to pay tribute and remember them. It was a lovely idea to collect these letters and messages because otherwise, they would have been washed away by the rain or destroyed and lost.

The presentation went really well and although I was probably the most nervous I have ever been for something like this, it couldn't have gone better. It is scary to speak in front of natives because I have done presentations in French before but only to either my fellow university students back home or to foreign Erasmus students like myself. However, this time, it was to French students so there was an added pressure to avoid any mistakes etc. But like I said, it went so well and they all seemed so engaged in what I was saying. Once I had finished, some students asked to have a look at my books and some even took the time to compliment me on my French. It was a great feeling.

I have more assessments next week, though no presentation which is a relief. Although, I do have some other presentations coming up in March and I am hoping to use this opportunity to speak about Brexit to French students as I'd like to give a native's personal spin on what is happening in the UK.

So, as you can see, I am well and truly back into the swing of uni life and despite the busyness and work demands, I am still enjoying the new semester. I'll let you know how next week's exams goes…

British vs French Universities
FEBRUARY 10, 2017

I came across this YouTube video where two people describe their experiences of studying in both British and French universities. What they said, couldn't be truer.

Have a watch to see the differences…

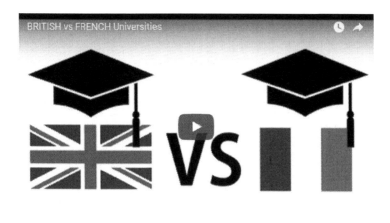

https://www.youtube.com/watch?v=9aIFuHqmY0o

The other side of the coin
FEBRUARY 11, 2017

I have tried to ensure that I stay well clear of politics on this blog and so, I tread with caution writing this post. However, with all that is happening in the world of politics, be it Brexit or Donald Trump's position on immigration which has upset the apple cart, we can see that the very notion of immigration never ceases to provoke a reaction.

I chose to call this post 'the other side of the coin' because the year abroad has given me a rare opportunity to walk in the shoes of an immigrant, which most people don't get the chance to do. And, as I watch the news about Trump's travel ban or hear the phrase 'take back our borders' in the Brexit debate, it occurred to me that I am an immigrant here in France, something that I never saw myself as.

I didn't flee from a war-torn country or use a boat to cross the channel, I just jumped on board a Eurostar train to set up a temporary life in another country. So, that makes me an immigrant even though, maybe, lots of people don't see me as such.

I suppose what this post is about, is that the year abroad lets you see the world and society through a different pair of eyes. I can't compare my situation to the refugees we see on the television but, what I can compare is my feeling of being a 'foreigner' in a new and sometimes daunting environment. It is often too easy for us to forget that behind every immigration statistic or number, there is a story. I imagine that I am now a part of France's immigration statistics even though I came to this country under very different circumstances than what we tend to envisage when we hear about immigrants.

So, while you may have the goal in your head to come back from your year abroad speaking fluent French or Spanish etc., the chances are that you will come back with something that you didn't anticipate. For me, the year abroad is more than what they might tell you it is at university. You come back with a different mind-set, a profound respect and better understanding of immigration.

Handball Match: Besançon 32 – Dijon 26
FEBRUARY 13, 2017

Yesterday I got the opportunity to watch a handball match between Besançon and Dijon at the Palais du Sports which is about a 10-minute walk from where I live.

I confess that I have never been to a handball match and so, no very little about the game. However, I was very pleased to be invited by a boy who I know from university to watch Besançon against Dijon.

The game started at 3:30pm but in order to get free tickets, we had to be there at 2:45pm. As soon as I arrived, it was very busy but it didn't take long to get in and find a seat with a good view.

I have the say, the atmosphere was electric. There was chanting, drums, trumpets and music played by a band. It was a fantastic ambience and you couldn't help but join in with shouting "allez, allez, allez" to support Besançon.

All our support seemed to work as Besançon won 32 against Dijon 26 – it was a tight game at first with Dijon doing very well before Besançon hit one ball into the net after the other.

The game was broadcast live on TV but I am not sure what channel and the next game in March will be against Paris.

So, I'd like to thank my friend for inviting me to a really enjoyable afternoon.

Have a good week whatever you have planned!

Speed doesn't always equal fluency
FEBRUARY 14, 2017

Before coming to France, I assumed that speaking French fast was an accurate demonstration of fluency. In some ways, I aimed for this. I wanted to speak French quicker and quicker because only then would I consider myself fluent. However, living here has made me realise how wrong I was…

As I have mentioned many times before, learning a language can be an uphill battle and speaking personally, you can set yourself unrealistic goals. My goal was to speak French faster because I thought this would make me sound more fluent. When in fact, I have learnt that it only makes you a bad communicator and speaking fast isn't something to strive for.

Maybe what I am saying is fairly obvious. In English, speaking too quickly has always been considered bad communicating but we all do it at times. I am terrible at speaking too quickly in English and then people have to ask me to repeat myself. But, that's English and so when it came to French, I never thought that I needed to slow myself down when I spoke. Instead, I wanted to get faster.

Though, since attending a French communication class, I have seen that speaking slower and making yourself clearer is much better than rushing through what you want to say. The class I go to is aimed at native French students who want to improve their written and spoken French. We have been doing work on developing our communication skills. One element was to speak slower and articulate words probably. The teacher often told the French students off for speaking too quickly. What's more, a key part of the presentation last week, was how well we spoke. Did we pause and let the listener absorb what we were saying etc? Did we take our time etc? I think often when we speak, we forget to take our time and sometimes this leads to misunderstandings.

Therefore, this lesson has been incredibly beneficial. I now speak much slower in French and English, making it feel more natural. I feel that in fact, it has made me more fluent because it allows me time to think of new words and avoids using meaningless utterances such as um or like or donc in the French case. So, my tip is: don't speak too quickly in French. Speak slower, pause more, take your time. This is much better for you and your language development. It is also regarded as better French!

A week of exams
FEBRUARY 17, 2017

Bonsoir to you all,

As you have no doubt gathered from the title, the majority of this week's lessons were taken up by exams.

The first exam I had, took place on Monday evening. I translated a text from French to English about Donald Trump – which can be found here if you want to read it.

http://www.europe1.fr/economie/etats-unis-sous-la-pression-de-donald-trump-les-constructeurs-automobiles-sorganisent-2945996

On Tuesday, I had three exams; a translation from English to French, an English business exam and then a French grammar exam. All of which seemed to go well.

On Wednesday, there were no exams so I just had my normal lessons.

On Thursday, I had another English to French translation exam.

The holidays start next week and I will be restarting university on the 27th February. Although it would have been nice to go home for the week, the fares were expensive and also, the week off gives me the chance to catch up with work and prepare for some more exams taking place at the beginning of March. I also have two presentations coming up in a fortnight.

During the holidays, I am planning to visit Strasbourg and go to a few museums in Besançon. I'll keep you posted…

Until next time!

Matt

Saturday Life
FEBRUARY 18, 2017

I love waking up on a Saturday morning and seeing a clear blue sky and the sun shining – it spurs you on to get out of bed and head outside. So, this morning, as I have done a few times, I went to a café in the city centre to indulge in a pain au chocolat and a café crème – (I learnt that café au lait doesn't actually exist in France, it is called a café crème despite the fact that the cream is milk and not cream). This is a nice little weekly treat!

After this, I went to the indoor food market, which is on the main Place de Révolution. I bought some chicken fillets from the butchers and because I am a student, I got 10% off so I only paid 3 euros 60. It is always worth having a look on the market because it can be cheaper than going to the supermarket and you can buy only what you need.

Just a short post, so bon week-end à vous tous!

Exploring 'Little' Germany
FEBRUARY 25, 2017

As I'm sure many of you are aware of my trip to Strasbourg yesterday, I still want to write a post to accompany the pictures that I posted on social media.
I chose the title 'little' Germany because out of all the places I have visited in France, Strasbourg felt the most different linguistically. You can see from the map below, it's a city that more or less sits on the German border and so, German seemed to spoken a lot there. At times, it did rather feel like a German city rather than a French. Another NTU student told me that they speak Alsatian there too which I didn't know. It was a real surprise to hear German being spoken fluently by French shop assistants and you could feel this merge of both French and German culture. In the bakeries, you would find French baguettes and also Pretzels.
I had some awkward moments at times because I would speak in French and then the shop assistant would reply to me in German or tell me the price in German, leaving me a little unsure what to say because I think they assumed I was German – not sure why!
Also, for me, this city had the most international feel out of all the places I've been to. There were shops such as Starbucks and Barclay's bank and even an Apple store. I haven't seen these brands in France before. Besançon is much more traditional French and so, there tends to be only French brands and shops.

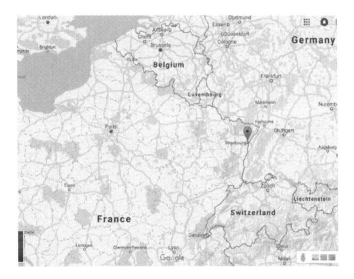

The journey there was fine, however, the TGV was delayed 20 minutes so, I was later into Strasbourg. I travelled on the local TER train to the TGV station and then changed to the TGV direct to Strasbourg. The train coming home was en route to Marseille, in the south of France. The journey was comfortable and relaxing. I love the views from the train along the way.

The trip to Strasbourg was enjoyable as I haven't had the chance to travel since being back from Christmas. It was nice to see another city and region and experience how different each corner of France is.

Long time no blog
MARCH 7, 2017

Sorry I haven't written a blog in a little while. Last week, I restarted uni after having a week off for the half-term. It was a busy week as I had three quite tricky exams; one on Monday, one on Wednesday and one on Thursday. All the mid-semester 2 exams are done now. I'll be soon getting ready to do the end of semester 2 exams which take place at the end of March and mid-April.

Today, I did a presentation about Brexit but in terms of how it was reported in the French right-wing press. It seemed to go okay and I had lots of questions afterwards. I hope they found it engaging. There are no more exams this week.

Next week, I have another presentation to do, again on Brexit, but this time, I am more presenting what happened. I am looking forward to this one because it is just in front of one teacher and it is more of a discussion rather than a presentation. I am looking forward to not having an audience watching me too!

So, that's the exams spoken about. In other news, I have been getting my teachers to sign a Module Assessment Form to take back to Nottingham to prove that I have attended lessons and exams. I had about 14 forms to get signed. They are all done now, except one but I have done my best to ask for it to be signed so there's not much more I can do. I have also printed out 13 forms for Semester 2 to be signed before I leave for Easter in April. Although I come back to France for two weeks after the Easter break, these two weeks will be used to pack and move out.

I think that's all to say. My mind feels like there is more to write but I think that's just because it's been a busy week or two!

Take care wherever you are

Make hay while the sun shines
MARCH 11, 2017

In almost two months' time, I'll be back in the U.K and my year abroad experience will be over; Besançon will feel like a distant memory. So, with that in mind, I wanted to get out and enjoy my surroundings while the sun was shining.

It seemed like most of France was basking in spring sunshine – Besançon reached 20c and maybe higher in the direct sun.

After my grocery shop, I sauntered down to the river to blow away the cobwebs. It's a pretty and tranquil part of the city where you can just hear the river streaming past. There are lots of little bridges to cross too, enabling you meanderer like the river to admire the environment from a different angle and under a different shade of light.

The walk took me right under the Citadelle before I turned around and headed back onto little side streets where the golden sunlight bounced off the walls and onto the cobbled path.

Another beautiful Saturday afternoon. Have a good weekend whatever you have planned.

Culture Shock
March 13, 2017

Before coming to France, I was warned about experiencing a 'culture shock' described in the dictionary as 'the feeling of disorientation experienced by someone when they are suddenly subjected to an unfamiliar culture, way of life, or set of attitudes.'

So, did I experience this?

The short answer is: No.

There is something quite scary about the word 'culture shock' and it provokes a fear of going on the year abroad. However, speaking personally, I never experienced a culture shock. Yes, life here is very different. The culture is not like that back at home but I never felt disoriented or as if I had been dropped onto another planet.

Maybe I'm lucky. Maybe others have experienced a culture shock. Maybe my situation has allowed me to adapt better to the environment. I don't know the reason but I find France and the French no more different to us British people. The French seem just like us. Don't get me wrong, I do crave home and some British culture but, that's just a bit of homesickness.

I think it depends on your personality as to how well you settle in and adapt. If you are used to being abroad and amongst different nationalities, I imagine life in another country will feel more familiar. Whereas, if you have never left your home country then, I guess you might be more likely to experience this dreaded 'culture shock'. Who knows?

I suppose the essence of this blog is, don't be afraid of being abroad. You will adapt and even if you do feel disoriented, it will soon pass once you mix and see that we are all humans living on the one planet called Earth!

The flower that blooms in adversity is the rarest and most beautiful of all
MARCH 24, 2017

It's Friday afternoon and so a peaceful time to look back on this week and think about all that has happened, not only here in France but of course back home in the UK.

The week soon changed after I learnt of the attack in London. And so, despite being in France, I still feel that this week comes to a sombre close and I wanted to convey this in my blog.

I had just got home from university when a notification popped up on my phone telling me of the first initial reports of a shooting outside Parliament. I quickly turned on Sky News, the only British news channel I can watch here. I followed the events all afternoon and saw some horrific images of the victims. At this moment, the UK seemed so much closer. I could feel the fear, the shock and the sadness in my room even though I wasn't anywhere near London.

London seemed a different city to how I am used to seeing it. It was grey. It was a city in crisis. The reporters had to shout to be heard above the sirens and the helicopters. Of course, everyone was calm on-screen but you could sense the panic in the air.

And, although the UK has felt like a second home since moving to France, I never stop feeling British. The attack left me feeling sad for our country, our city and our people. I was sad for the innocent people who suffered because someone tried to destroy the home of democracy and our nation which is beacon around the world because of the values we hold.

This week comes to a close, leaving a huge sadness and void in our society. So, before I carry on my blog, I would like to say that we lost some brave souls on Wednesday – my deepest condolences to those families who have lost their friend or family member.

The flower that blooms in adversity is the rarest and most beautiful of all

I have around two weeks left before I hope to come home for Easter. Lessons have been quite intense again as we get ready to start the final exams that start next week and end on the 12th April.

On Wednesday evening, I was invited to watch a film about a village in Alsace that is completely self-sufficient. They grow their own fruit and vegetables, make their own flour for bread and even produce their own electricity. It was an interesting night and it was followed by questions from the audience to the mayor of the village. It seemed to get quite heated at times and people had the microphone taken off them.

I have also used this week to distribute the forms I need to be signed by the teachers to take back to NTU.

Spring in my step
MARCH 31, 2017

Good afternoon from a very warm and sunny Besançon! It's been a glorious week in terms of the weather. We have had a clear blue sky every day this week and on Thursday, it reached 26 degrees!

Last weekend, I went to the centre commercial in Besançon city centre where there is a H&M, Superdry, Footlocker and other well-known brands of clothes shops, to buy some t-shirts so that I was ready for the hot weather that was expected.

The week at uni went well. It was the last week of lessons as next week, the exams start. On Tuesday, we had some students from the lycée (high-school) in some of our lessons as they were spending a day at university to see uni life and what kind of lessons they might want to choose when they leave school. They call it '24 heures dans le supérieur' (24 hours in university). In France, students don't seem to choose a degree course like we do back in the UK, they choose lessons from all different kinds of subjects.

In the other lessons, we have been preparing for next week's exams and going over anything we didn't understand.

So the schedule for next week:

On Tuesday, I have 3 exams

On Wednesday, I have 2 exams

On Thursday, I have a presentation and 4 exams.

I hope to write once they are all completed to let you know how they went. Take care and passez un très bon weekend!

Nearly at the finish line...
APRIL 8, 2017

Good Morning!

Well, what a week it has been! Waking up and realising that it was Saturday was a very nice feeling this morning!

As I mentioned in my last blog 'Spring in my step,' this week was all about exams.

Tuesday: I had 3 exams. The 1st exam involved writing a business email in English. This was fairly straightforward and the only difficult thing about it was translating the French so that I knew what to write in English. There were some other English grammar tasks too.

The next exam was translating an extract from a novel in English to French. This for me is probably the hardest form of translation. However, overall, I was happy with what I had written. There were some French grammar questions in this test too, such as conjugating all the verbs into the passé simple.

The last exam on Tuesday was the exam for Erasmus students. This involved grammar questions and also a 250 essay in French. We were given 3 topics to choose from. I chose to write about whether not voting in elections is dangerous for democracy. I really enjoyed writing this. Overall, I was happy with how I did but as with all exams, you can never really trust your instinct.

On Wednesday, I only had 2 exams. The 1st exam was later on in the afternoon at 4-5pm. I had to translate 15 sentences into English. Then, I had to make my way down to the other university site, about 10 minutes walk, to do another exam.

Then, I had to make my way down to the other university site, about 10 minutes walk, to do another exam. This exam was quite fun. We watched an extract from a film and had to talk about it shot by shot. I love analysing films so this module has really suited me. The exam lasted until 7 pm but I finished around 6:30 pm. The film we analysed was an old 1950s American film called Sunset Boulevard. In every shot, we had to write down things such as the camera movement/angles, all the technical details we had learnt and also analyse the shots. There were some questions too about the history of cinema.

Thursday was the busiest and most tiring day. I had a 15-minute presentation in English about the film 'The Big Lebowski'. We got given this film at random. Again, just like the exam, we had to talk about it shot by shot and analyse it. The extract we were given was only 1 minute long. I was really pleased with how this presentation went. We had good feedback too.

The next exam was at 2-3. In this exam, I had to do some French grammar tasks and also write down 5 French regions and departments. I then had to pick one and write about it. Again, I think this went well.

At 3-4 I had a translation to do from English to French on an article written in the Guardian.

At 4-5 I had to get quickly down to the other site to do the final exam of the day which was a translation from French to English.

So, a busy week all in all. I only have 2 more exams left to do next week and then semester 2 has finished! I can't believe how quickly it has gone! In total, excluding the Easter break, I have only 3 weeks left in France.

Taste Test
APRIL 13, 2017

Good afternoon all, what a beautiful day it has been again in Besançon!

Yesterday, I officially finished semester 2! All my exams are now done so I can look forward to getting back to England for the Easter break. I can't believe it's been 4 months since I was last home…

I had 2 exams yesterday – one starting at 8 am and another one which started at 1 pm. I have to say, they weren't the easiest exams and I didn't come away feeling that I had done a great job but we will just have to see or as the French say – 'on verra!'

This afternoon I got an email from a teacher, telling us that we could collect the exam we did for her last week. I thought it would be a good idea to pick it up before the Easter holidays so I collected it and found out my marks. The marking system works very differently here and everything is out of 20. The pass mark is 11 and above. The system of marking and grading we have in the UK like 2.1 and firsts etc, doesn't exist in France.

After collecting the exam mark, I headed home and walked through t the main street to enjoy the glorious weather. As I was walking, a lady stopped me and asked if I wanted to complete a questionnaire about food. I said yes, but explained I wasn't French so she would have to bear with me if I didn't understand. Luckily, I did understand and all was fine. To be honest, it was a rather strange and bizarre thing to happen. She took me to this rather 'posh' hotel which I didn't know existed. She sat me down by a computer and said that I would be trying some cheese, ham and saucisson.

Out came three plates of different cheese. I had to try each one and then answer questions on the computer about each one – rating taste, texture, smell etc. Then, she brought out three plates of ham and I did the same thing and also for the saucisson. It was a surreal experience. I have always wanted to do taste testing so I found it rather fun. It all just happened so quickly and out of the blue. I think the products were either new and needed to be tasted by the public before going into the shops or the products had been out in the shops and the companies wanted to know what people thought of them.

I know tomorrow is a bank holiday in the UK, it's not in France so I hope everyone has a good Easter weekend. I hopefully will be back on UK soil in 48 hours!

Home Run
MAY 2, 2017

I arrived back in France yesterday after spending two weeks back at home in England. I had such as nice time being back there. I was sad to leave yesterday morning but at the same time, I knew that I was going to be back home for good in two weeks! I can't quite believe that my year abroad comes to an end in just 12 days!

People might wonder why I even came back to France if I only have two weeks left. Well, when I booked the Eurostar tickets, I wasn't sure if I would have exams in May so I decided to come back just in case until I knew for sure. There was talk of some exams taking place in May and so, I was glad that I would be coming back just in case. Thankfully, I don't have any exams now to do so I am using the time to get ready to come back to the UK for good.

Also, being back in France means that I can collect any exams and grades from last semester. Not only that, I need to meet with my coordinator who will sign off all my assessment forms so that NTU can see that I attended the lessons and exams.

The journey back yesterday was really easy. The Eurostar left St Pancras at 11:30 am and I arrived in Paris Gare du Nord at 2:50 pm French time. I always travel by metro so I wanted to try to take the number 65 bus to Paris Gare de Lyon so I followed the signs but ended up completely lost. Eventually, I found the Gare du Nord again and took the Metro RER D to Paris Gare de Lyon. The time I got there, I only had an hour to wait so I grabbed some food from Pret à Manger and waited for the TGV back to Besançon. At 4:30 pm I checked the departure board and the platform was showing so I went straight there and got my seat. The journey was relaxing and I soon arrived in Besancon at 7:20 pm. Since it was a bank holiday, the buses weren't running so I took a taxi which was waiting outside the station back to the campus. It was only 12 euros for the journey.

So, that's it. The next few days I will be packing and clearing away the things in my room. I am going to give some the kitchen stuff I bought to the Erasmus Student Network who distribute all the things to next year's Erasmus students. I also need to meet with the cleaner who will check my room before I leave otherwise you will be charged 40 euros.

Adieu la France…What an experience!
MAY 14, 2017

To be sat on the TGV heading to Paris to catch the Eurostar back to the UK is surreal to say the least. I can't quite believe that my year abroad or rather the 9 months in France have come to an end. It has been an incredible experience for many reasons and one that will stay with me for a long time.

I can vividly remember the day I came to France in September 2016. It was a daunting prospect coming to live here, not knowing what to expect or even if I would be able to cope with living in a foreign country for most of the year. I was sad to put my life on hold back in England and start a new, somewhat scary adventure alone in France. However, with the help and support from my family and with every passing month, Besançon soon became somewhere I felt at home.

I chose Besançon because I knew little about it and I wanted to discover somewhere different. I am so pleased that I made the decision to come here. It's a perfect size for an international student, not too big nor too small. It has a town and village feel about it and I especially like the market that takes place weekly, bringing local farmers and their produce to the town. This was the type of traditional France I really wanted to see. Besançon was a fantastic place to live and study and it will take time getting used to not being there.

Before setting out to France, I had several goals in mind that I wanted to achieve during my time in France. One being, of course, to improve my French. And, without a shadow of a doubt, my French has come on leaps and bounds since September. However, I also realised that although improving my French was an important aspect of the year abroad, the year abroad is not just about that. For me, this year abroad has been about learning about myself. It has revealed to me that I have more strengths than maybe I had first thought. Personally, this year abroad has taught me about my personal development and all that I can achieve. Yes, I still have more to learn and develop in myself, but ultimately, these 9 months have given my time to see just what I am capable of, rather than what I am not.

I have grown in confidence, knowing that making mistakes is inevitable but these are crucial to the process of learning and developing. There were times when self-doubt creeps in and you wonder whether you are making any progress towards your goals, but actually, when you leave the situation and look back, you can see just how far you have come. Often, you only see yourself making small steps rather than giant leaps of progress but these small steps, whatever they are, are what shapes you and your time away. There were very few negatives to my year abroad, but for all the times I felt lonely or homesick or doubted my ability, I wouldn't change these times. They have given me good lessons and taught me to appreciate the tiny pleasures in life that can frequently go unnoticed.

I am grateful for this unique opportunity to study in France and witness daily life in another country. I am particularly grateful for the times when I have been able to reflect and think about what my nationality means to me. Seeing the UK and life for that matter from the continent has allowed me to question what it means to be British. Living in France has allowed me to look at the UK with a fresh pair of eyes. Despite its imperfections and its struggle to find its place in the world, I have learnt that the UK will always have a special place for me because it's home. Some may try and undermine our nation, but I know that our country is a shining example to many. We may face difficult times, but our values will always make sure we 'keep calm and carry on'. France has taught me to be proud of my roots and for me, it's time to stand up and wave our flag.

The year abroad has been an incredible eye-opener and an amazing experience for many reasons. People have asked me whether I'd do it all again. The short answer is…no, I wouldn't. I think that, although I had a great time, and I would not change a thing, this opportunity cannot be repeated because it's one of those things that you can only do once. It requires a lot of your energy but it also provides you with so much fulfillment. For me, what I have learnt and how I have matured in 9 months is beyond what I could have anticipated. The maturity that I have reached can sometimes take a whole lifetime, but I have had to grow and mature in 9 months.

So, I wouldn't do it again but for sure, I would recommend it. It's been a fantastic adventure, none of which would have been possible without my coordinateur who was always on hand to help me. However, crucially, my family's support and love has been my continued guidance. Their wisdom and advice kept me going. I owe all this to you, you never stopped encouraging me.

And finally, my girlfriend. Words won't quite do justice for what she has done for me. Her unconditional love is beyond anything I could have asked for. She has supported me every step of the way. I don't know what I would have done without her.

Thank you for reading, thank you to you all for being there. France and Besançon, it's been a pleasure. Adieu/farewell!

Printed in Great Britain
by Amazon